Anonymous

**Danville Riot**

Anonymous

**Danville Riot**

ISBN/EAN: 9783337307875

Printed in Europe, USA, Canada, Australia, Japan

Cover: Foto ©ninafisch / pixelio.de

More available books at **www.hansebooks.com**

# DANVILLE RIOT

## NOVEMBER 3, 1883.

---

# REPORT

OF

# COMMITTEE OF FORTY

WITH

## SWORN TESTIMONY

OF

## THIRTY-SEVEN WITNESSES, &C.

---

RICHMOND:
JOHNS & GOOLSBY, BOOK AND JOB PRINTERS.
1883.

# REPORT OF COMMITTEE OF FORTY.

*To the Citizens of Danville, Va.:*

The Committee of Forty, charged, by your resolution hereto subjoined, " with the duty of thoroughly inquiring into all the facts, and preparing for publication a true and full statement of the causes and circumstances which led to the riot " in your town on 3d November, 1883, "and also a statement of the conduct of the people during the period from the occurrence of the riot to the closing of the polls on the 6th day of November," respectfully and unanimously reports that on Monday, 12th November, 1883, the committee organized and appointed proper sub-committees, and by publication in the *Daily Register* requested all persons having information of the matters to be investigated to appear before the sub-committee for taking testimony at the office of F. F. Bowen, notary public, and testify as to such matters.

That said sub-committee for taking testimony attended regularly at the office of F. F. Bowen, from Tuesday morning, the 13th November, till Wednesday, the 21st of November, inclusive, during which time thirty-seven witnesses, after having been first duly sworn by F. F. Bowen, notary public, deposed before said sub-committee. The witnesses so deposing were, for the most part, known to the committee personally, and represented all classes and avocations among our citizens, including two policemen, one white and one colored, who were present at the riot, and exerting themselves to quell the same.

All of these witnesses, whose names are signed to their depositions herewith submitted, as a part of this report, are known to the citizens of Danville, and will be recognized as intelligent and thoroughly reliable.

lated except by the wounding of one of the special police while on duty Saturday night, by a shot fired from behind the house of a negro man.

(3). That from within one-half hour after the commencement of the riot the town was completely under the control of the Sergeant and his police force, and that no further disturbance of its peace and good order, except the shooting of the special policeman, as stated above, occurred, and that such peace and good order continued to prevail up to and including the day of election; that sundry prominent citizens prepared and caused to be printed and circulated, on the day preceding the election, a circular, signed by themselves and by the Superintendents of both political parties, guaranteeing to each and every citizen, without regard to color or party, the free and undisturbed right of voting; that no violence, threats, or intimidation whatever was shown towards negro or Coälition voters, but, on the contrary, such voters were repeatedly assured by citizens, policemen, and military officers sent to Danville by the Governor of the State, that they would be protected in their rights to vote as they chose; that the election day was quiet and without any disturbance or difficulty at any precinct or elsewhere in the town, and the election itself honestly conducted, and free and fair in all respects; and that the negroes as a body refrained from voting under the advice and command of their party leaders, while others voted the Coälition ticket without hindrance from any quarter.

Your committee has thus confined itself to the investigation of the facts and preparation of the statement required by your resolution, and herewith submit the evidence as a full and complete vindication of our town and people from "the gross misstatements which have been circulated through a portion of the press of the country."

W. T. SUTHERLIN, Chairman.
L. C. BERKELEY, Jr.
W. P. BETHELL.
BERRYMAN GREEN.
H. J. MILLER.

H. H. HURT.
T. L. SYDNOR.
W. H. WHITE.
J. T. AVERETT.
R. W. PEATROSS.
R. V. BARKSDALE.
ABNER ANDERSON.
JNO. M. JOHNSTON.
E. H. MILLER.
S. I. ROBERTS.
ROBERT BRYDON.
FLETCHER TURNER.
R. F. JENNINGS.
SAMUEL S. BERGER.
E. B. WITHERS.
H. HIRSH.
W. S. WILKINSON.
R. C. HERNDON.
THOMAS D. STOKES.
JONAS KAUFMAN.
CHARLES ORCHARD.
J. R. PERKINSON.
T. B. FITZGERALD.
WM. C. GRASTY.
H. F. VASS.
JNO. G. FRIEND.
JNO. R. PACE.
P. W. FERRELL.
J. L. TYACK.
T. R. SCLATER.
GEORGE C. AYRES.
J. M. NEAL.
JNO. F. RISON.
W. H. TROWBRIDGE.
JAMES FRICKER.

# EXHIBIT A.

---

## Meeting of Citizens.

A large meeting of citizens was held at the Opera House this morning in response to the following circular:

### MEETING OF CITIZENS.

The citizens of Danville are requested to meet in the Opera House at 9 o'clock to-morrow (Saturday) morning, to consider the propriety of adopting resolutions returning thanks to our fellow-citizens in other localities who have expressed their sympathy and their willingness to aid us, if necessary, during the recent riot in Danville, and also to appoint a committee who shall prepare and publish a full account of the affair and the causes that produced it.

MANY CITIZENS.

At this meeting Colonel E. B. Withers was requested to procure an organization, and on his motion, Dr. H. W. Cole was elected chairman.

Messrs. J. T. Averett, P. Bouldin and Abner Anderson, member of the press, were appointed secretaries.

After some preliminary remarks suitable to the occasion, Major W. T. Sutherlin offered a series of resolutions which, with some slight modifications, proposed by General H. H. Hurt and Judge Berryman Green, were as follows:

*Resolved,* That we the white people of Danville, in mass meeting assembled, do return our heartfelt thanks to our fellow-citizens of other cities and towns of Virginia, North Carolina and Maryland, as well as friends in various sections of the country, who in public meeting and otherwise expressed sympathy for us in the riot which occurred in our streets on the 3d day of November, and who generally proffered us their aid if needed on that occasion.

*Resolved,* That in view of the gross misstatements concerning that riot which are being circulated through a portion of the press of the country, misleading the public mind as to the facts of the same, this meeting do hereby appoint through its chairman a committee of forty, who shall be charged with the duty of thoroughly enquiring into all the facts and preparing for publication a true and full statement of the causes and circumstances which led to it, and also a statement of the conduct of our people during the period from the occurrence of the riot to the closing of the polls on the 6th day of November.

The resolutions having been unanimously adopted, Judge Green suggested that editors and correspondents of newspapers ascertain and publish to the world the name, position and character of "C. M.," the correspondent of the *Whig,* who has published through that paper such grossly false statements of the occurrences on Saturday evening last, and this proposition was received with applause.

The chairman appointed the following as the committee under the resolutions, and in appointing them was careful to select a number of citizens of Northern birth :

W. T. Sutherlin (chairman), L. C. Berkeley, W. T. Bethell, Berryman Green, H. J. Miller, H. H. Hurt, James Fricker, T. L. Sydnor, W. H. White, J. T. Averett, R. W. Peatross, R. V. Barksdale, Abner Anderson, J. M. Johnston, E. H. Miller, S. F. Roberts, Robert Brydon, Fletcher Turner, R. F. Jennings, S. S. Berger, E. B. Withers, H. Hirsh, W. S. Wilkinson, R. C. Herndon, T. D. Stokes, J. Kaufman, Charles Orchard, J. R. Perkinson, T. B. Fitzgerald, William C. Grasty, H. F. Vass, J. G. Friend, J. R. Pace, P. W. Ferrell, J. L. Tyack, T. R. Sclater, George C. Ayers, J. M. Neal, J. F. Rison, W. H. Trowbridge.

On motion, the meeting adjourned.

H. W. COLE, *Chairman.*

J. T. AVERETT,
P. BOULDIN,       } *Secretaries.*
ABNER ANDERSON,

The deposition of W. J. Dance and others, taken before F. F. Bowen, a notary public in and for the corporation of Danville, Va., on the 13th day of November, 1883, to be used as evidence by a committee appointed by the citizens of Danville under the foregoing resolutions of said citizens in meeting assembled— Exhibit A :

W. J. Dance, being duly sworn, deposes and says:

I am 21 years old, reside in Danville, and live with Ruffin, Woolfolk & Blair. The difficulty between Noel and Hense Lawson, when I first saw them was at the lower window of my office. My attention was attracted by hearing a white man say, "Stand back." I went to the door and saw Hense Lawson, and a white man on each side of him. Neither Noel or Lawson had any weapon that I could see; I know neither of them had anything in their hands, in sight. Besides myself, when I first got there, there were only two white men present; there were about 125 or 150 negroes present. I locked up the back door, and then picked up a gun which had been left there that day, and went to the front door. Each of the two white men there besides Noel had pistols in their hands, and ordered the crowd of negroes not to interfere in the fight between Noel and Lawson; that they were having a fair fight. When I first got to the door I saw about five or six negroes, with drawn pistols. Afterward Mr. Lea said, "He (Noel) has beat him (Lawson) enough," and told the policeman to take the negro away; and Bob Taylor took Noel away from the negro, and Noel went away up the street to wash the blood from his hands. After the negro had gotten off, they (the white men and negro police) tried to disperse the crowd of negroes, but they refused to go, and said that they had as well have it out right there. In the meantime a message had been sent down to the Opera House, where the white men were holding a meeting, to come up—that there was going to be a difficulty. Some 10 or 15 white men had come up before the firing commenced. My office is on the north side of Main street. The white men were in front of my office and the office of J. E. Catlin, on the pavement and in the gutter. The negroes were in the street in front of them from the middle of Catlin's office down to the front of Henry Vass' store. The white men, after seeing that they could not disperse them, said, "We are ready for you—if you won't disperse, we'll settle it." A negro jumped up in the crowd, and held up a pistol, and said, "Damn you, come on." Then the firing commenced I don't know who fired first. When the firing commenced, I saw thirty or forty pistols in the hands of the negroes. I don't remember seeing any white man, of the ten or fifteen who were there, who did not have a pistol. Between six and ten shots were fired by the colored men, so far as I could see, in front of my office. The negroes ran when the firing commenced, and soon I could not see any. There were about three shots fired by the negroes, as they ran from Jere Nicholas' store-corner. At the time of the commencement of the firing there were present about 350 or 375 negroes and about 15 or 20 whites. I did not see the scuffle between Geo. Lea and the negro, but the negroes rushed up and wanted to know what "damned scoundrel fired that pistol." Some of them pointed to Bob Taylor and said, "There is the damned scoundrel;" and some to Geo. Lea and said, "There is the damned scoundrel." Geo. Lea said, "Yes, I am the man." Then they said that they had to have the thing out, and just as well have it out there.

And further this deponent saith not.

W. J. DANCE, Jr.

Ro. Lipscomb, being first duly sworn, deposes and says :

I live in Danville, and am telegraph operator of Western Union Telegraph Company. I heard one negro, whose face I know well, but do not know his name, say on Monday night that the negroes were not going to vote in Danville; that they had been instructed, in the meeting, from which he had just returned, not to vote.

And after this the deponent saith not.

RO. LIPSCOMB.

Chas. D. Noell, being first duly sworn, deposes and says :

As I was passing down Main street, Saturday, 3d November, 1883, about half past one, walking rapidly, I passed two negroes in front of H. D. Guerrant & Co.'s store, not knowing who they were ; and this negro, whom I afterwards learned was Hense Lawson, came near knocking my left foot from under me, when I turned and asked him what did he do that for. His reply was, in a very insolent manner : "I was getting out of the way of a lady, and a white lady at that." I replied that that was all right, and passed on about three paces, when the negro with him replied that it didn't make a "damned bit of difference whether it was all right or not; he can't do anything about it"; and the negro Hense Lawson repeated the same thing. I turned and struck the first speaker, when they both struck me and pushed me from the sidewalk. I recovered, and beat them back to the store wall. By that time I suppose twenty negroes had gathered around, and not a white man was present, as they were at dinner. The crowd began to gather around, and these two negroes began to draw their pistols—that is, made a motion as if they would draw them. I don't remember definitively, but I may have put my hand around to see if I had my pistol; but I did not have it. I left the scene and went home to dinner, where I expected to have a buggy and horse to meet me at two o'clock, to go to the country. The horse and buggy was late coming up. I drove down the street and stopped at the Opera House, went in and spoke to George Lea. He asked me about the difficulty I had had, and wanted to know if I intended to do anything further about it. I replied that I thought it would be best if I did not, as so many negroes were on the street; that it would be best not to create any excitement; that it would end in something serious. I came out in my buggy and drove up in front of the Arlington, intending to stop at Steinruck's, when some one, standing on the corner, hailed me and said: "By God, here I am." He repeated it three times, and in a very defiant manner. I made no stop, but turned short round in the street, and as I passed down the street, I glanced back and saw he was gathering up a crowd and coming on down Main street on the sidewalk after me. I drove, rapidly down to the Opera House, got out and gave the horse to a negro boy. I went up in the Opera House and told George Lea that that rascal had insulted me again and I wanted him to see that I had fair play, when he and Bob Taylor immediately got up and followed me. When we got in front of Averett & White's store, I noticed that this negro, with fifteen or twenty others, were standing in front of Ruffin, Woolfolk & Blair's office; they did not stop until they saw us coming. The eyes of most every negro in the crowd was directed to me, as I came up, as if they were expecting me. I halted in front of the negro Hense Lawson and asked him what he meant by calling at me on the street. He said he didn't call at me. I told him that he did, and struck him (I had told Mr. Lea and Robert Taylor that I would not strike him with anything but my fist). The negroes commenced to crowd around. Mr. Taylor and George Lea drew their pistols and told them to stand back and allow fair play. I had the negro in the collar and was pummelling him when I saw the negro, said to be George Adams, slip up behind George Lea and tried to wrench his pistol from his hand, and in doing so threw him down. Mr. Lea held to the pistol ; the negro fell, I think from a lick from a cane by Mr. Taylor, and when he got up Mr. Lea's pistol fired— whether accidental or not I don't know. A dozen negroes, I suppose, said : " It was a fair fight and Mr. Noell whipped him ; now you all go off." The crowd began to disperse. I went over to Hamlin's store with two friends to wash my hands; they told me I had better go, as my being so bloody would create an excitement. While I was up stairs in Mr. Hamlin's store washing, the firing commenced. I ran down, and as I ran in the door some one ran over me and knocked me away, and before I could recover the doors were closed.

And further this deponent saith not.

CHAS. D. NOELL.

---

14th November, 1883.

The witness, W. G. Lynn, being sworn, deposes and says :

I started from home, in the northwestern part of the town, on Union and Floyd streets, Saturday, 3d November, 1883, about 3 o'clock, and in coming down—about half the distance—I met eight or ten stout negro men going up that way. I soon after returned home and notified my family of the riot and returned again as fast as I could walk, and the same men passed me armed with guns, clubs, and pistols ; they were returning to the street. When I arrived on the street everything was quiet. I saw nothing or heard 'no fuss. These negroes passed me again and stopped at " Hell's Half Acre."

And further this deponent saith not.

WM. G. LYNN.

---

P. Bouldin made affidavit that the account of W. E. Sims' speech, as reported in his paper, herewith filed and marked " P. B.," is correct :

SIMS' SPEECH—"P. B."

Friday morning a notice was scattered over town that W. E. Sims would speak in Danville that night, in front of old post-office, in answer to the Danville circular. As the Democratic Club was to meet in the same building, and suspecting the inflammatory nature of the address which was contemplated, the owners of the building objected to his speaking there. When the time came, therefore, the negroes adjourned to the Courthouse yard. A little before eight o'clock, Mr. A. M. Wheeler rose and spoke about ten minutes, simply urging his hearers to keep quiet on the day of the election, not to go armed to the polls, nor do anything calculated to produce trouble. Having finished his remarks, he left the stand, and, we presume, went to his office.

Squire Taliaferro then rose and spoke, to kill time until the orator of the day arrived.

When he concluded, Sims arose amidst the shouts of at least five hundred negroes. He stood on the steps of the Courthouse with a large torch-light before him. The negroes were packed closely round him, and only about fifteen white men could be seen on the outskirts of the black crowd, and they were Democrats, who went to see and hear what was going on. The writer was one of them, and, we must say, it was a horrible spectacle—one lone white man standing up amidst a vast crowd of Africans, who were yelling and whooping at the top of their voices, and at night.

He rose with the famous Danville circular in his hand, and the first thing he did was to read the names of the signers, twenty-eight in number, men of highest standing and universally respected. He commenced by calling them all liars. Then he began to read the circular by paragraphs, commenting as he went, and trying to answer the charges. "Another lie," he would say, at the end of each sentence. About every ten minutes, for the space of an hour, he pronounced the men who signed the circular liars, and every time he did it the negroes applauded.

His object seemed to be to inflame the minds of the negroes against those gentlemen, and to stir up a bad feeling between the rich and the poor. He ridiculed most of the signers of the circular, as if to set their colored hands against them, and some of them he charged with the most rascally conduct. Not satisfied with abusing those whose names were on the paper, he went out of his way to attack other good and honorable white citizens. He said the circular contained forty-five lies, and that the men who endorsed it knew they were lies. When he finished reading and commenting on the document, he read the names of the twenty-eight signers a second time, saying they were all a set of "liars, scoundrels and cowards!"

Just think of it! A speaker denouncing in that style twenty-eight of our most respected citizens, and the negroes yelling their applause with hellish delight. Can anything be imagined better calculated to bring on a row? And yet those white Democrats who heard the diabolical harangue and heard the shouts of the negroes stood it; and they did it for the sake of peace. It was a great wonder that some man, inflamed by the insults offered to him and his friends, did not offer violence to the speaker. Had he done so a bloodier scene would have followed than that which was enacted on the following day.

Thanks to the high sense of duty of our law-abiding citizens and their love of peace, they bore it all, and not a hair of Sims' head was touched! Moreover, they permitted him to get in a buggy with James Verser and drive out of town the next day unmolested. They knew if any one of them had attacked him that it would in all probability have resulted in a general fight between the whites and blacks. We are glad it so happened, as it places our men in the right.

---

The witness, W. P. Graves, being duly sworn, deposes and says:

I was in the club-meeting on night of Friday, November 2d, 1883, and stayed until it adjourned. L. Stovall and myself came out after adjournment, and were waiting for Raine at Wiseman's corner, when he proposed to walk around where Sims was speaking to hear what was going on. When we got there I suppose there were 12 or 15 white men and about 500 negroes present. Sims was reading the circular, "Coälition Rule in Danville." He called the names of all the signers and denounced them as liars, scoundrels and cowards; these denunciations were repeated throughout his speech; almost every sentence was wound up with "that's a lie, and they know it." I never have, in all my life, heard such a speech, and I hope to God never to hear another such. It was the most incendiary one I ever heard. The negroes were yelling applause at every sentence. Johnston, the mayor, came up then and told me there was likely to be a riot, and he wanted me to assist him in suppressing it—that he would do anything in the world I said. He insisted very much that I should go on the stand with him, and that he would make Sims apologize. I told him there was no danger of any row there. He was very strenuous in insisting that there would be a row, and I broke loose from him and came away, bringing all the white men I saw, to prevent any difficulty. I think I brought nearly all the white men away who were there. Mayor Johnston said he did not approve of Sims' speech at all; and the speech was what he seemed to think would produce the riot. The negroes were very much excited. He would read such sentences, and comment upon it, and say that is such a one, and the negroes would yell; and by their conduct showed that they were very much excited, especially when anything was read bearing upon the negroes. It was the vilest speech I have ever heard. It seemed that he was trying to get up a row, and I had no idea of accommodating him. After we left, I and, so far as I know, all the white men, went home.

WM. P. GRAVES.

———

J. C. Reagen, being first duly sworn, deposes and says:

I was on Main street Saturday, 3d November, 1883, when the riot commenced. I did not see the fight between Noell and Lawson; but after it, as I came out of the Opera House, I saw the negroes crowded around a few white men in front of Ruffin, Woolfoolk & Blair's. One of them pointed to Bob Taylor and said: "There's the man who did the shooting, and he's got his pistol now." Taylor showed his pistol, and said: "Here it is." Some others showed theirs, and the negroes showed theirs likewise; and just then one fired (I don't know whether white or black), and the firing became general. The negroes had said that they had as well have it out there as anywhere. The policeman Withers tried to get them to disperse and they would not. After the firing commenced I don't recollect anything else. I suppose there were 150 or 200 negroes there and about 15 white men.

J. C. REAGEN.

———

J. E. Perkinson, being first duly sworn, deposes and says:

I first heard a noise as if parties were in a fight. I started from Waddill's store down toward Ruffin, Woolfolk & Blair's, where a crowd was collecting to witness the fisticuff between Noell and Lawson. I stood there awhile and asked Noell how he was hurt; he was bloody, and I thought he was cut. Noell started back to wash his hands; I started after him, but came back in front of Chatelain's store, and while I was standing there the crowd of negroes were pressing around the white men on the pavement. The white men were trying to get them to disperse. One negro said, "There is the man who did the shooting." Taylor opened his coat at and pulled out his pistol and showed it to them. While standing there some one said, "Fire." Who it was, whether a white man or negro, I know not. I then turned, and as I turned the negroes were running up the street, and I saw about five or six of them firing, as they ran, at the whites. I then made for Paxton's store, and got as far as the door. I was unarmed, and I turned as I got to the door, attracted by Walters Holland, as he was carried up the street. I followed him until they took him into Guerrant's store. I did not see any more of the firing, as it was about over then. I saw white men firing—ten or fifteen; I don't know who they were. I suppose there were from one hundred to two hundred negroes and not over twenty whites present.

J. E. PERKINSON.

---

B. F. Williamson, being duly sworn, deposes and says:

When Noell and Lawson first commenced the fight, Geo. Adams, a colored man, was standing in our store paying us some money. He ran out and across the street to where Geo. Lea was standing with a pistol, and slipping behind him he grabbed it, when they had a scuffle, each trying to get possession of the pistol. Adams got Lea down on the ground, and in the scuffle the pistol went off. The negro jumped up and ran off, and in a few minutes he came back to the crowd of negroes and tried to urge them on Lea, and was cursing, saying "there's the damned scoundrel who had the pistol I tried to get, and if I had gotten it I would have shot him." He was trying to get the negroes to attack. There wasn't over fifteen white men present, and about one hundred and fifty to two hundred negroes. Before the fight between Noell and Lawson was over there were 500 negroes present. Noell had no stick or weapon in the fight. I don't know how the firing commenced, but the cursing by Adams was going on when it commenced. I saw lots of negroes with arms.

B. F. WILLIAMSON.

---

Frank Corbett (colored), being duly sworn, deposes and says:

I was up town when the fuss commenced. I was with Hense Lawson and Davis Lewellin Saturday, 3d November, in the morning at about 11 o'clock, and went in the billiard room of Brown with Hense Lawson. Mr. Joel Oliver was in there, and he and Hense Lawson had some words. I took Hense and carried him out into the bar-room. I told him to let Mr. Oliver alone, that he would get into some fuss; he said he did not care if he did, that he was ready and had plenty of friends to back him. I talked to him awhile and left him. I got down to the store, and soon saw him and Davis coming down the street. He met Mr. Noell about Ruffin, Woolfolk & Blair's office, and stepped on Mr. Noell's foot. Mr. Noell asked him why he did it. Hense said he was getting out of the way of a lady, and Mr. Noell said it was all right. Davis said, "If it ain't all right, I can make it all right," and he and Noell had a fight. They hit about four licks apiece. Mr. Noell left and came down the street by Mr. Vass' store. I do not know where Lawson and Davis went. I heard it rumored around that there would be a fight, for two or three weeks.

FRANK CORBETT.

---

T. E. Gregory, being duly sworn, deposes and says:

I was on the street Saturday, 3d November, about three o'clock. I came down from the Opera Hall. I saw Jeff Corbin standing out in the street. I saw a negro with a pistol, as I thought, aiming for Jeff, and I made for him as quick as I could. About that time the firing commenced. I think the negro fell over, but he got up and started again; I don't know what became of him afterwards. I saw about a dozen pistols in the hands of negroes, and I saw several fire them. I saw white men with pistols, too; but I do not know who they were, white or black. There were between 250 or 300 negroes present, and very few whites (15 or 20.)

T. E. GREGORY.

---

W. A. Meeks, being duly sworn, deposes and says:

I had heard that Noell and a negro had a difficulty on the street, and had tried to find out about it, but could not. When he passed by I asked him, and he said, Come on up here; and I went up with him to Ruffin's office, and met Hense Lawson, with two or three other negroes. I could not hear what he said to Hense. Lawson made some answer, and Noell commenced to strike him with his fist. A yellow negro was boisterous and commenced hallowing murder. No one had touched him. I told him to shut up, and he said he would not do it; afterwards they got quiet for five or ten minutes. I heard a pistol go off, and in a few minutes after that the firing commenced. I saw a negro in the crowd with a pistol above his head.

W. A. MEEKS.

15th November, 1883.

**J. G. Miller, Sr.**, being duly sworn, deposes and says :

The first I saw or heard of the riot was when the first fight commenced with Noell and Lawson, who were engaged at that time, and when neither had any appearance of blood or wounds inflicted upon them; who were fighting, each one without any weapon of any kind that I could see, in the presence of a few white men, not over three or four at that time, and not many colored persons. As the fight continued the number of persons (both white and colored) present increased, until there were ten or a dozen white persons and a hundred or more colored persons, about which time the fight between Noell and Lawson was concluded by Lawson's hallowing "enough," as I understood it. During the fight of Noell and Lawson, from the time that I first saw them, three white men, with their pistols drawn, stood very near and around Noell and Lawson, who were fighting. A large number of colored people were standing immediately in front of them, in the street, looking on. After the fight between Noell and Lawson was over, a colored man ran forward at one of the white men, who had a pistol in his hand, and both fell on the sidewalk together. Immediately after falling, the colored man jumped up and ran back, when a pistol was fired, by whom I do not know. After which another white man went into the midst of the crowd of negoes, who informed me his object was to disperse them, whose efforts were unsuccessful. In a short time after which more white men came up, and very soon thereafter firing of pistols commenced, which was soon over, as the colored people dispersed as rapidly as they could until the streets were cleared at that point. I was standing about sixty feet from where Noell and Lawson were fighting when the firing commenced ; there were one hundred and fifty or more negroes present and fifteen or twenty white men.

J. G. MILLER.

---

**J. T. Morton**, being duly sworn, deposes and says ;

I was in the Opera House when the riot commenced. I heard they were fighting, and got down as soon as I could. I started up the street and got to the upper corner of Averett's shoe-store ; and I saw, I suppose, 10 or 15 shots, some from one side of the street and some from the other. One ball from the opposite side from Market Square struck Averett's shoe-store about 3 feet above my head, and the brick-dust fell down on my hat. I went across Main street and up to Wiseman's corner; when I got there, there were two shots fired from the direction of down Union street. I could not tell where they came from. I think about that time the firing ceased. I saw Cabell and Judge Aiken in the street trying to stop it. I suppose there were 150 negroes present when the firing commenced; there were not more than 25 white men on the street. I saw a negro with a pistol in his hand, saying, "It had as well come now as Tuesday—let them shoot." The negroes were shooting as well as the white men. I saw it was a riot good.

J. T. MORTON.

---

L. L. Bass, being duly sworn, deposes and says:

I was in the Opera House when the riot commenced and looked out of the window. I saw two negroes shoot towards the white men and run, and one of them shot over his shoulder back toward them as he ran. I saw only one of them with a pistol. A white man came down and went to Jopling's to get arms. This is all I could swear to. I heard a man tell a negro he had started the fuss and he had better get away. Col. Cabell, I think, told him not to hurt the negro.

L. L. BASS.

---

S. F. Terry, being duly sworn, deposes and says:

I saw across the street about 10 o'clock Chas. Noell walking off and a negro picking up his hat. I did not see any licks passed; about two hours afterwards I saw the fight between Noell and a colored man, and saw a negro grasp a white man's wrist and try to take a pistol from him; the pistol went off. I saw Mr. Peter Booth trying to get the crowd of negroes to disperse, but they seemed determined and pressed forward. Soon the firing commenced, and some of the negroes ran through our store (Hamlin & Hinton's), and one ran by me with a knife with which he cut my finger accidentally. I think that at least 150 negroes were present when the firing commenced, and not over 20 white men. I saw no negroes with arms save the one with the knife. I saw one white man standing in his door with a double-barrelled gun. These are the only ones with arms I can swear to.

S. F. TERRY.

Chas. Friend, being duly sworn, deposes and says :

I went down to the Opera House to open it for Mr. Jamerson· The crowd come, and Col. Cabell desired two of us to keep the gallery, to keep the colored people out. Geo. Lea, Bob Taylor, and myself were the ones to go up there, and just as Mr. Barksdale finshed reading the circular on Coälition Rule, I heard a disturbance in the street. I went to the window and looked out, and saw a crowd of negroes rushing across the street in three or four directions towards our office (R. W. & Blair's). I could see, from the window, a white man and negro grappling together. I thought them boys at first. ⁚I did not leave just then, because I thought it would be over in a minute; but when I did go down, which I did in about five minutes, Dance was standing in the office-door with a gun, and a crowd of negroes were standing jam up to the sidewalk. He seemed excited, and told me Chas. Noell had just beaten a negro severely, and to go to the Opera House and tell them all to come out. I went down, and Col. Cabell seemed anxious to keep the crowd together. I hallowed to them that the thing was about over. I left the Opera House again with Mr. C. G. Holland, and going up the street I saw that things were much worse ; and when I got between N. & Hessburg's and Vass', some of the darkies in the crowd commenced cursing at me pretty lively, and I went into our office and went behind the safe and got an old pistol, which had been returned to me the day before. I went out again, and then I heard a negro holler "damn you, this thing has got to be settled, and we had as well settle it now." He was standing in the middle of the crowd. A white man, with a large pocketknife, stepped out and hollered, "Here's at you," and then I heard a shot, which, in about a second, was followed by a volley from both sides. The negroes ran, some of them firing back as they run. My pistol could not be cocked on account of rust. I think about three hundred negroes were present when the firing commenced, and about twenty whites.

CHAS. FRIEND.

16th November, 1883.

N. F. Reid, being duly sworn, deposes and says:

The night W. E. Sims was speaking here (the night before the riot), I was standing on the outskirts of the crowd and heard C. E. Hawkins, colored (on the market), say in a loud voice : "Let them pitch in, if they want to ; we can give them enough of it." I heard a good deal of talking around among them, as if they were mad and would like to fight. Sims said he had come there to answer the circular composed of "148 lies." After commenting on it very severely, he said the man who wrote it knew he was writing a lie, and that it was gotten up by George Cabell and his pimps; that it was lies from beginning to end, but Cabell had too much sense to sign it. It was the most incendiary speech I ever heard. After he read the circular, he read out each name signed to it, and commented on each name in rough terms, and said that every man that signed that paper, signed it knowing it to be a lie, and he was a liar, coward and a scoundrel; and told the colored people that they need not be afraid of them, that they were liars and cowards; and he said it was democratic principles to shoot a man in the dark, but if they would come openly to him he wasn't afraid of the whole damned set of liars. He would call on the negroes and ask them if they didn't know that these were liars; and they said: "Yes, yes." Mayor Johnston and Jim Verser were present, and both said they could not endorse such a speech. Johnston proposed to Capt. Graves to go up and make Sims apologize and modify. Jim Verser said the same. I saw the latter part of the riot as I came down from the Opera House, and I saw two negroes shoot as they ran off.

N. T. REID.

The night that Poindexter, from Louisa, spoke here, about a week before Sims' speech, Squire Taliaferro (colored) said in his speech that the Virginia gentleman had been talking about negro rule, and that, if negro rule would cause Danville to sell a few more pounds of tobacco, they were going to have it; and that, by God! they were going to have half negro rule anyhow, and that they did not want any more North Carolina people here anyhow.

N. T. REID.

---

James P. Harrison, being duly sworn, deposes and says:

About 2 o'clock on Saturday, 3d November, 1883, I went from my office to the Opera House, and finding, as I thought, that it had not been opened, I started up the street to get the key. As I passed Grey's shoe store four young negroes were seated on the stone window sill, and one of them said as I passed, "There goes old Jim Harrison," adding some very insulting language, which I did not listen to and cannot remember; but his tone and manner was exceedingly insolent, and calculated to have excited a disturbance with most men. After this, finding that the Opera House was in fact open, I returned and went to the mass meeting. It was a very full meeting of white men. In the midst of the business some disturbance on the street caused a rush to the windows, and it was reported that a negro had been shot. The chairman and prominent men present urged the assembly to keep quiet and finish the business before they went on the street, and only a few individuals left after this request. A large majority of those present remained until the resolutions were passed, and afterwards went upon the stand at the request of the chairman to sign them personally. There was no adjournment until the firing had ceased. Myself and Colonel Cabell left a majority of the meeting behind us when we came out on the street, and when I ran across to get a pistol at Jeppling's store the shooting was entirely over and the street cleared of negroes. From that time the efforts of all the white men seemed to be to preserve the peace and prevent further trouble. As soon as I got a pistol I came up in front of the Arlington Hotel. An excited crowd was there, and in a few minutes, under the advice of Col. Cabell and Judge Aiken, the Sergeant of the town had ordered out the Danville Grays, who filed out from their armory and were stationed at different points on Main street. Very soon the Sergeant commanded the crowd to disperse and go home, and the crowd obeyed.

On Monday afternoon, as I came down town, several negroes accosted me near Steanfield's store and asked me what would happen to them if they went to the polls on Tuesday. I told them that they could vote without any trouble; that I and other white men were determined that everybody should have a fair showing. One of them told me that their leaders had advised them to vote at Wimbish's, but not to vote in Danville. On several other occasions negroes told me that the colored men had resolved not to vote, and were not going to vote in Danville. On Tuesday, finding that the negroes were not voting in Danville, and that the Coalition judges of election were not serving, I went to A. M. Wheeler's house, he being the acting superintendent of the Coalition party in Danville and P. M. I asked him why he and the other judges did not serve. He told me that from the first he was doubtful whether he could serve, and Dr. Green had advised him not to serve because of his wife's exceeding nervousness; but that W. P. Robinson and W. H. Graswit, who were Coalition judges of election, had come to him to advise with him whether they should serve or not, saying that they did not see any use in their serving, since their people were not going to vote. He told them that they ought by all means to serve, but they persisted in the contrary opinion on the grounds stated. I also asked him why the negroes were not voting. He said he did not know; that three had come to him that morning, and he told them to do as they chose, that he did not think there would be any trouble. I then told him that we understood the negroes were advised not to vote. He said I never so advised them; and then told me that on Sunday he had been sent for in the revenue office to confer with his party leaders, and that Pleasants and Payne advised that they should advise the colored people in the town and in the county to stay away from the polls, since they could not possibly carry it anyhow. He disagreed with them, but they insisted.

JAMES P. HARRISON.

---

R. M. Hubbard, being duly sworn, deposes and says:

I was in the Opera House when the disturbance first occurred on the street, and the superintendent persuaded the people to remain until the business was finished. Quiet was restored there. A few moments after, some one at the window said we had all better get out here, and the crowd made a move again to get out, and were quieted a second time, a few only going out. The firing pretty soon commenced, and most of them went out, I suppose, although I left a majority in the house, and when I got down the shooting was about over. I saw negroes with pistols about Market street, and a negro was looking back, with a pistol, apparently about to fire back. I think I saw ten or twelve negroes with pistols. The Grays were called out in a few moments, and the crowd requested to disperse, which they did. I was put on guard that night as special police, and had been riding around town and beyond the Dry Bridge. Mr. Geo. Coleman, L. Stovall, P. Gravely and myself were quietly riding along, when we were fired into from the yard of a colored man just beyond the Dry Bridge, and I was wounded in the leg, and my horse was a so wounded. I suppose twelve or fifteen shots were fired into us. We replied after they fired the second time; we stopped after the first fire and asked who it was and what it meant, when they replied with another volley. I returned and came back to Danville, being badly wounded.

R. M. HUBBARD.

## November 17th, 1883.

James Wood, being duly sworn, deposes an l says:

I have lived in Danville since 17th July, 1865. I am now Sergeant of Danville, and have been three years or more; was nominated on the Coälition ticket and endorsed by the people generally at last election; had no opposition. On the 3d November, 1883, I was sitting in my office and heard several pistol shots in quick succession, followed by a volley of shots. I went as fast as I could travel to Main street, a distance of one square from my office, where I found the citizens, generally, assembled in large numbers on Main street. As soon as I could comprehend the situation, I called upon the citizens to listen to me, and in the name of the Commonwealth of Virginia, I commanded peace, being sheriff of the town, and immediatly called upon the Danville Grays to parade and fall into line and aid me in preserving the peace. After doing which I disposed of the men as I thought best, stationing them at different cross-streets with orders to disperse all crowds of persons assembled on the street. My next action was to close all drinking houses in town and to summon a posse of citizens in addition to the military force, to perform guard duty and such other duty as the exigency might require. The citizens, generally, responded, and assembled in the armory of the Grays, where they were organized and placed under different squad commanders. I had the Grays under my command, and the crowd dispersed within half an hour after the riot. The crowd, generally, dispersed upon my command to them to do so, some remaining, that were removed from the streets by the orders of the military. Many of the prominent citizens aided me in restoring order, and but for their aid I could not have succeeded as well. The citizens, generally, were obedient to my orders, and seemed law-abiding and anxious to preserve the peace.

From this time on until the close of the polls on election day, either in command or in conjunction with Mayor Johnston, he and I exerted ourselves to insure quiet and peace to the citizens and a quiet and peaceable election, and this was secured to all the citizens of the town, so far as I know. I assured all persons that felt any apprehension on that score, that there was safety, and that I would go with any who were fearful. A more quiet and peaceable election I have not seen in Danville. In my opinion, there was entire safety to all to go to the polls and vote as they desired, although I met colored persons who professed that they were afraid to go and vote, and I assured them there was no danger. I was at the Courthouse precinct most of the time, and at Woodson's some, and in sight of the other precincts, they being all. I saw no one threatened, or any violence at or near the polls, or anywhere. I saw no display, at any precinct, of guns or fire-arms of any sort.

On Saturday, about 6 o'clock P. M., I received a telegram from Governor Cameron, saying he had heard of trouble in Danville, and wished to know the facts. I replied that the town was in great excitement, and that four persons (I thought) had been killed, but that now the town was under control of the civil authorities and quiet. On the same night Governor Cameron telegraphed me to advise him of any change, and if any help was needed to let him know.

On Sunday about 12 o'clock M., Mayor Johnston and I, out of abundant caution and to relieve the Grays, who had been on duty since Saturday afternoon, telegraphed Governor Cameron to send a company of military from Lynchburg before night. He replied by asking if there was any new exigency, or if any change had taken place. I replied, "No, no new exigency, but out of abundant caution, and to relieve the company here on duty." These telegrams were all on Sunday. Then I received one on the same day from Governor Cameron, suggesting a division of my company into reliefs, saying that from the tenor of my telegrams he thought that a posse of citizens would be more effective than troops, and declining to send any unless advised by me of their need, and telling me to so advise him at once and fully of any change in the situation. I had no further communication from or with him until Monday night between 8 and 9 o'clock, telling me that he had sent the troops—a section of artillery and a company of infantry. Then, in reply to that, I said to the Governor that the excitement had greatly subsided since mine and Johnston's telegram to him asking for troops, and that the town was now quiet, and I did not deem it necessary that he should send the troops, but that he could do as he thought necessary. The troops arrived here early Tuesday morning, and I stationed them at the armory of the Danville Grays. They remained there, subject to my order, and there being no need for them, they were not called upon at all. They remained here until Wednesday morning, and left about 10 o'clock. There was no time between the riot and the end of the election that my authority as Sergeant of the town and conservator of the peace was suspended or incapable of being enforced. So far as my observation extended, I saw no disposition to commit any violence or renew the difficulty by any one. Rumors, almost numberless, were constantly coming to me and others who were engaged in preserving the peace of indications of further disturbance, but when investigated were found to be groundless, except one case, where the special guard was fired upon by some unknown person on Saturday night near the Dry Bridge, when Mr. Hubbard, one of the guards, was wounded, and also his horse.

JAMES WOOD, Sergeant.

---

H. A. Cobb, being duly sworn, deposes and swears:

I was up in the Opera House Saturday, 3d November, 1883. Some disturbance occurred on the street. I came out before the general shooting. When I reached the street I saw a large crowd of negroes on the street in front of R. W. & Blair's and a few white men on the pavement, when I heard some one, I think a negro, as it came from the direction of the crowd of negroes, say, "We can shoot as well as they can;" and almost immediately the firing commenced. I can't say which side fired first. There were about 200 or 250 negroes and 15 or 20 whites. I saw several pistols in the hands of negroes and white men also; both parties seemed to be ready. I got into the door of the office of R. W. & Blair, and remained until the shooting was over, when the colored people left the street.

I was in town from the riot until the close of the polls Tuesday. I was a special policeman at the polls that day from sun-up to sundown. On the day previous to election I was asked by several colored people if there would be any difficulty about their voting, and I told them, No; I would be there, and would guarantee them the right to vote any way they wished.

I saw no fire-arms or guns on that day, save those the policemen had. I was on duty at Woodson's, 3d ward. I saw a negro there with tickets—Coalition—offering them to any who wished to vote, and some few negroes voted. The election was entirely quiet.

H. A. COBB.

---

Mason Arrington (colored), being duly sworn, deposes and says:

Saturday, 3d November, about half past 12 o'clock, I was in H. Jones' barber-shop, when I heard Squire Taliaferro, leader of the negroes and a former policeman here, say, "There will be a difficulty here this evening." While eating dinner at the factory of

Arnett & Wemple, where I work, I heard the hands say that if any one had touched Mr. Sims that they would have taken up for him and fought for him.

I voted on the day of election. It was as quiet as I ever saw. No one attempted to interfere with me at all.

HIS

MASON ✗ ARRINGTON.

MARK.

---

November 19th, 1883.

P. B. Booth, being first duly sworn, deposes and says:

I heard a portion of W. E. Sims' speech, on Friday night, 2d November, 1883. He held up a paper in his hand, and said here we would read a parcel of lies gotten up against "you people"—against negro rule in Danville. I could not begin to say what he did not say. I think it the most outrageous speech I ever heard, and calculated to incite a row—to influence the negroes to attack the whites. At the close of almost every sentence he denounced the white men, and the negroes would yell.

Late in the evening, about three o'clock, Saturday, 3d November, 1883, I was in my store, attending to my business as usual. From the crowd in the store going to the door, I knew there was some excitement on the street. I went to the door and saw on the opposite side of the street from the house a white and colored man fighting. I immediately went across the street to where it was. There were only a few white men present, and at that time there were about 100 or 150 negroes crowding on the few. I tried to disperse the negroes, and they refused to go. A negro about that time grabbed at a pistol in the hands of a white man and tried to wrench it from him, and in the scuffle for the pistol the pistol was fired. The white men were trying to keep the negroes back, so that the white man and negro should have a fair fight, as he said. The negroes fell back a little when the pistol was fired, but soon crowded up again, and several of them, pointing their fingers to the white man, said: "There's the rascal that shot." I again urged them to disperse; they still refused, and one negro said, in a loud voice: "Let them come, damn them; we are ready for them"—he holding his hand at the same time behind him, from which I believed he held a pistol in his hand. About that time the firing commenced, both negroes and whites shooting. I saw negroes, as they ran, fire back at the whites, and I saw them fire before they ran. I suppose between forty and sixty shots were fired in all by both sides. Some of the whites fired over the tops of the houses as the negroes ran. I was made special policeman Monday morning following. Order was restored immediately after the riot. There was no further disturbance anywhere. I was on duty from Monday to Wednesday morning, and during Tuesday I visited all three of the polls. I never saw a more quiet election anywhere. Outside of the police I saw no display of fire-arms anywhere. I saw a colored man at each precinct with Coali-tion tickets, distributing them. I saw J. B. Ralston, Internal revenue collector, get one and vote it. I saw a great many col-ored men and told them go and vote, that there was no danger; they said they did not want to vote. I asked some of them if they were afraid to vote, and they said, No. I was unarmed when I went across to the fight; it was about thirty yards from my store. I suppose there were present, when the firing commenced, about 12 or 20 whites, and about 200 or 250 negroes.

P. B. BOOTH.

---

W. J. Moore, being first duly sworn, deposes and says :

I heard a part of W. E. Sims' speech on Friday, 2d November, 1883. He held up a paper purporting to be a circular from the people of Danville to the Southwest and Valley, on negro rule in Danville. He stated one article after another contained in that circular was a pack of lies, and called each name and firm signed thereto, and stated that they would go before the country as per-jured men ; that he (Sims) was here to denounce these men as "liars, scoundrels and cowards," and urged upon the negroes to go to the polls on the day of election prepared to assert their rights at all hazards; that the people of Danville were cowards, and would not fight. I consider it one of the most incendiary speeches I ever listened to, even in the days of Reconstruction, and calcu-lated to excite the worst passions of the negroes, and they ap-plauded him to the echo. He was heartily endorsed by the negroes. From the time of the riot until after the election I saw no attempt by anybody to intimidate the colored people. On the contrary, on the day of election, I saw a number of negroes go to the polls and receive tickets from one of their party, fold them and place them in their pocket, and walk off and not vote.

W. J. MOORE.

Chas. G. Freeman, being first duly sworn, deposes and says :

I am a member of the regular police of Danville, and have been on duty for more than a year. On Saturday, 3d November, 1883, I was on duty on Craghead street, and heard of the fuss on Main street; hastened there and found, I suppose, forty or fifty whites and about three hundred negroes. I did all I could to disperse the crowd. Mr. Joel Oliver told the negroes if they would disperse the whites would. While trying to disperse the crowd a negro showed me his pistol, and said they had not been treated right, and that they intended to have their rights. In a moment the firing commenced, but I know not who fired first. I saw negroes and whites both firing. Some negroes would whirl and fire as they ran, and whirl and fire and again run.

I was on duty Saturday night and Sunday morning. Order was restored in half an hour after the riot, and the town was in the hands of the police-military under the orders of the Sergeant. Saturday night was the most quiet one I ever saw in Danville. I was at one of the polls election day, and everything was perfectly quiet. I distributed circulars issued by Mayor Johnston, urging the people to come and vote.—Ex. " C. G. F., 1 "; also the circular Ex. " C. G. F." herewith filed.

CHAS. G. FREEMAN.

---

" Exhibit C. G. F."

NOTICE.

We, the undersigned, law-abiding citizens of Danville, determined to keep the peace, have met and conferred together, and we assure all persons, white and colored, without regard to party, that we desire nothing but a fair election on the 6th day of November, and we pledge every one our word and faith that we will use all of our power and influence to see that every citizen exercises his right to vote without being bulldozed or intimidated.

JNO. D. BLACKWELL,<br>
GEO. C. CABELL,<br>
J. H. JOHNSTON (Mayor),<br>
A. M. AIKEN,<br>
L, C. BERKELEY, Jr.,<br>
JAS. P. HARRISON,<br>
BERRYMAN GREEN,<br>
J. D. BLAIR,

L. E. HARVIE,
JAMES WOOD (Sergeant),
H. W. COLE, (Coroner),
M. P. JORDAN,
E. KEEN, Jr.,
R. C. HERNDON,
J. F. RISON,
WM. E. BOISSEAU,
J. J. PRITCHETT,
JNO. A. SMITH,
T. L. BROWN,
P. H. BOISSEAU,
PHIL. L. GRASTY,
W. S. WILKINSON,
T. R. McDEARMAN.

Representing, under authortity, our respective political organizations in Danville, we approve the foregoing spirit and sentiment, and pledge our parties to use every effort to sustain the same.

A. M. WHEELER, City Central Com.
J. B. RAULSTON,
GEO. C. CABELL, Chm. Dem. Party.

———

"Exhibit C. G. F. 1."

PROCLAMATION.

MAYOR's OFFICE,
*Danville, Va.,* Nov. 5th, 1883.

*To the People of Danville:*

All good citizens deprecate the present disturbed condition of our town, and earnestly desire the restoration of peace and good order. For the promotion of their so proper wishes, I have appointed eleven special constables in each ward, who will be under the command of chiefs as follows: In the First ward, Capt. Harry Wooding; in the Second ward, J. M. Covington; in the Third ward, P. H. Boisseau. The special constables in each ward have been appointed upon the recommendation of their respective chiefs, and are all reliable men. And I have also called into service the Danville Grays as the military coädjutors of this special constabulary. This arrangement will go into effect this day (Monday) at 10 o'clock A. M.

So complete and reliable is this arrangement for the preservation of peace and the protection of the town, that I feel fully warranted in assuring my fellow-citizens that peace and good order will be maintained ; and I, therefore, call upon all good citizens to resume their usual avocations ; to cease appearing upon the streets armed with shot-guns or other weapons, and thus, and by quiet conduct and conversation—"the things which make for peace"—aid and assist me and the other authorities of the town in restoring peace and good order, as all good citizens should do.

J. H. JOHNSTON, *Mayor.*

E. Keen, Jr., being first duly sworn, deposes and says :

I was in the Opera House, 3d November, when the firing commenced. I heard ten or twelve shots fired before I got down the steps, and when I got down the firing continued, and just as I got up to the crowd the negroes scattered. I saw ten or twelve shots fired from the midst of the crowd of negroes, by negroes. There were about half dozen balls in the walls of the buildings in rear of the position the whites occupied, which must have come from the negroes who were in front of them. When I got to the corner I found about a dozen white men and a street full of negroes. Quiet was restored pretty quick after the riot, and order prevailed until after the election. I heard of no disturbance except that on Saturday night, when Special Policeman Hubbard was shot, while on duty, by some unknown person in a colored man's yard near Dry Bridge. I visited two of the polls Tuesday and everything was perfectly quiet. I saw no one with arms save policemen. I heard Capt. Booth ask four or five negroes if they were afraid to vote, and they said, "No."

E. KEEN, JR.

T. B. Fitzgerald, being first duly sworn, deposes and says :

I am contractor and builder, and one of the proprietors of the Riverside Cotton Mills. I live in North Danville, and was not present at the riot, and know nothing of it save from hearsay. Immediately after the riot I went across the upper bridge, on my way home, and met quite a number of colored persons coming towards town with their guns.

In North Danville, where I was from the time of the riot until Wednesday, it was quiet, and the most quiet election was held I ever saw. There was no disorder. Every citizen could have voted without hindrance.

T. B. FITZGERALD.

Dr. M. E. Douglass, being first duly sworn, deposes and says :

I reside in Danville, and am a practicing physician, and was in town on the day of the riot, but was not there at the beginning, and know not enough of it to make a statement. I do a large practice among the negroes, and attended several of the wounded, and all the deaths I know of resulting from the riot is four. Tuesday, the day of the election, a colored man named Geo. Peters came into my office for medicine for his child. I asked him where he was the day of the riot. His answer was, " I was in Chatham and didn't get home until last night " I then asked him if he was going to vote. He answered, " No, sir." I said, " You have been told not to, haven't you ?" His answer was, "The first thing I heard on stepping from the cars was not to vote."

I was here on election day riding all over town. I heard no intimidation ; I saw several pistols ; they may have been with special police ; I did not know the special police. The election was quiet. I take little interest in politics, and never voted but once before in my life. I came here from Philadelphia. I have been here nearly four years.

M. E. DOUGLASS, M. D.

W. R. Taylor, being first duly sworn, deposes and says :

On Thursday, the first day of November, 1883, I was coming back up the street with a friend, between 7 and 8 o'clock P. M. There was such a crowd of negroes on the corner of Main and Union streets that we had to pass single through them. I saw a negro make a gesture at my friend's back, and when I passed myself I looked back over my shoulder to see if it was repeated, and the same negro struck at my back. I turned and looked him in the face, and he shrunk into the crowd, I said nothing and passed on to the "Arlington " corner, when I heard a negro in the crowd call out, " What in the hell was he looking back about." I replied that was my business, but he could find out if he wished to meddle with it. I then saw a negro take a pistol from his hip pocket and place it in the side pocket of his overcoat, and start across the street to me with his hand still in the pocket with the pistol. Mr. James Covington then stepped up and spoke to the negro. saying, " this thing has gone far enough," also saying to me, " Bob, control your temper ; if we have any difficulty here we want it to be after the election." I then told the negro to leave at once, or else I would make him ; he then went back to the crowd and I went home. This negro I afterwards recognized to be the same one with which Charlie Noell had a fight on Saturday, 3d of November, two days later.

On Saturday, 3d of November, 1883, I went to the Opera House at half-past two o'clock P. M., where I saw Chas. Noell, who told me and Mr. Geo. Lea, who were alone in the gallery, that a negro, on his way to dinner that day, had stepped on his heel on Main street, and when asked what he meant by it, replied that he was getting out of the way of a white lady. Noell said, "of course that's all right," and stepped aside himself. As soon as the lady passed another negro standing by, said he "didn't give a damn if it was not all right," whereupon Noell struck him and ran him off the sidewalk ; then the two negroes together shoved Noell over into the gutter, when he recovered and started at them again ; they both backed and placed their hands on their hip-pockets. Noell, seeing no white men, said he passed on to dinner. We then, Lea and myself, asked him if we hadn't better go with him to see those youngsters; he said no, that he wanted things to be quiet until after the election, when he intended to flog that negro for insulting him. He then bade us good-bye, saying his buggy was waiting for him to go to the country. He had not been out more than five minutes, when he came back and told us that this negro, in company with several others, had hailed him as he passed the Arlington corner, and said, "damn it, I am ready for you ; here I am," and cursed him again. Noell said that was more than he could stand, and that he wished Lea and myself to see that he had fair play ; that he wished to give him a good dressing while he was at it. We went out with him and met this negro, in company with twenty or thirty, half-way between the Opera House and the Arlington corner. Noell turned to the negro saying, "This is the scoundrel who insulted me before dinner, and also hailed and cursed me as I was going up the street in my buggy just now." I then recognized this negro to be the same one I had seen with a pistol and had some words with on Thursday evening at the Arlington corner, as before related, and I demanded of him what he meant by it and related the conversation between him and myself. He stated that it was none of my "damned business" ; then Noell stepped out in front of him and they struck at each other about the same time. After two or three blows being passed they caught each other in the collar, when a colored man—I don't know his name—took hold of Noell ; I struck him across the arms with a cane I had and told him to stand back, that we intended to have a fair fight and that no weapons were to be used; whereupon he turned and ran down the street some distance, crying "murder" at the top of his voice. There was already quite a crowd of negroes, and they seemed to be coming from every direction. Not more than twelve white men were on the ground at the time.

In a few seconds one of the negro police, I think Adams, came to the spot and said: "My God, gentlemen, what is the matter?" I told him to try and keep the crowd back; that it was a fair fight, and no weapons being used. He said he would have to part them. I told him, then, to take hold of the negro, and I put my hand on Noell's arm and told him that would do. Adams took the negro into the barber shop, I think, and about that time Lea called for me. Upon turning, I saw him upon his knees, with both hands on his pistol, and a large negro man, I didn't know who, trying to wrench the pistol from Lea's hands. I struck the negro across the neck and shoulders with my cane, upon which he broke and ran, tripping me as he endeavored to get off, I not knowing whether it was accidental or not. That instant Lea's pistol was fired. I think the firing was accidental, as it was a double action pistol. The two parties engaged in the fight retired from the scene to wash themselves. About three minutes afterwards Hense Lawson, which I found afterwards to be the name of the negro engaged in the fight with Noell, appeared on the street by my side, when a negro in the crowd asked him what was the matter. He said, some white man had hit him in the face; he didn't know what his name was. In the meantime three policemen, Withers, Adams and Freeman, were doing all in their power to disperse the crowd, which was every moment increasing and pressing in; and several negroes in the crowd making loud complaints and threats, saying that they had been mistreated, and said they intended to have their rights, and that was as good a place to settle it as they could get; also exhibiting their pistols. I don't know how many there were, but I saw several; and some one, a colored man, pointed to Lea and myself, saying: "There are two of the damned rascals. We can shoot as well as they can. Shoot them." In a few seconds the firing commenced on both sides. The negroes soon broke and ran, but several of them fired as they retreated. I heard several balls pass very near to me, discharged by the negroes' pistols, and young Holland fell at my side as he turned to step upon the sidewalk. The ball was bound to have come from the direction in which the negroes were when the general firing commenced. When I noticed, I suppose there were about 12 or 15 whites present; the street seemed to be pretty full of colored people—I suppose 300.

I was under the charge of Mr. John Lea from Saturday night until after the election doing guard duty as special policeman. I saw or heard of no violence except when special policeman Hubbard was shot. I visited two of the polls, 1st and 2d ward; every thing was perfectly quiet, and several colored men passing backwards and forwards around and about the polls, but not voting.

On the day before the election I was ordered by John Lea, chief of special policemen, to disperse several crowds of colored people, and several colored men said, when requested to go home or to their places of business, that they intended to go there and stay all next day (election day).

W. R. TAYLOR, Jr.

Walter S. Withers (colored), being duly sworn, deposes and says:

I have been a policeman in Danville about 16 months. I was not on duty the day of the riot. As soon as I heard of the difficulty on the street I went down there. The fight between Noell and Lawson was over. There were about 25 whites on the pavement in front of R. W. & Blair's office, and 75 or 100 negroes in the street in front of them; they were still coming up of both colors. I tried to get the crowd to disperse. I went up and down in the crowd of colored folks and asked them to disperse, that they would create a disturbance. I said, "Why don't you all disperse? you will get hurt here." They said, "We don't intend to be run over." I told them it would be for their good to leave. I said, "Well, if you won't leave, I can't help it; I have done all I can do to get you to leave." At that time me and Mr. Jeff Corbin were together; he was trying to get them to disperse too, and Mr. Peter Booth hallowed to me to make them leave, and I told him I was trying to do it. I saw there was no use in trying to get them to leave, and stepped on the sidewalk at the lower end of the crowd of white people. Some gentleman in the crowd said, "If you all don't go away from here you will be hurt." At that time the firing commenced. The white people shot up in the air at first as if to scare the colored people away; then the firing seemed to be on both sides right at each other, and I stepped into Mr. Blair & Woolfolk's office, it was so hot. I staid in there about two minutes until the firing was over.

I was on duty from that time until after the election. I did not vote, but was not afraid to vote. I was at the polls, and everything was quiet. I heard of or saw no intimidation. I saw white men trying to persuade colored men to go and vote, promising them to go with them and see that they should vote as they pleased. I saw that prominent citizens of the town tried to calm the crowd after the riot. Order was restored immediately, and I saw or heard of no disorder afterwards, except I heard that Hubbard was shot near Dry Bridge Saturday night.

W. S. WITHERS.

The foregoing depositions were taken, subscribed and sworn to before me in the day above mentioned.

F. F. BOWEN, N. P.

November, 20th 1883.

Abram Wimbish, being first duly sworn, deposes and says:

I reside half a mile from the corporate limits of Danville. I was in town and attending a meeting of the citizens at the Opera House when the riot occurred. When I got down on the street the riot was over; I heard one or two shots as I reached the bottom of the steps. Four-fifths of the crowd was behind me in the hall when I came down. The civil authorities got control of the town in half an hour and quiet was restored. The white people yielded at once and submitted to authority; the negroes had left the street.

I was one of the judges of election at Wimbish's precinct, about three-quarters of a mile from the corporation limits of Danville. The election there was perfectly quiet and a full vote polled; there were about 62 white votes and about 330 negro votes polled. There was no disturbance there of any kind, no fire arms exhibited and no sign of intimidation.

A. WIMBISH.

Geo. W. Swain, being first duly sworn, deposes and says:

Friday night, November 2d, about 7.30 o'clock, while passing through Union street, going in the direction of the court house, I was overtaken by Mr. Epp Barksdale, and as he passed me the large crowd of negroes assembled in front of the court house by the speaking of Col. W. E. Sims, were loudly hurrahing, upon which some comment was made by myself to him, in substance that they yelled lustily, &c. He replied, "Yes, I'll be damned if we havn't got you. We have the white men of the Southwest with us and we have got the negroes solid against you, and I'll be damned if we can't turn them loose on you in five seconds." With this remark he pressed on and went up in the midst of the above mentioned crowd. Mr. Epp Barksdale is an active Coälitionist of Danville.

I have been voting for the last fifteen years, and have seen no quieter election than the one held on the 6th of November, 1883. Saw or heard of no intimidation or disorder. The town has been under control of the civil authorities from immediately after the riot until the present time and law has prevailed.

GEO. W. SWAIN.

L. J. Berkeley, Jr., being first duly sworn, deposes and says:

On Sunday evening, November 4, 1883, the Advisory Committee of the Democratic party of Danville, appointed Mr. R. W. Peatross, Col. E. B. Withers, myself and I think Mr. J. E. Schoolfield, a committee to wait on Col. J. B. Raulston and Maj. A. M. Wheeler, the persons recognized by our party as the leaders of the Coälition party in Danville, and expressed to them our desire and the desire of our party to preserve and enforce the peace of the town, and to guarantee to all citizens a fair and quiet election. We called on Raulston and Wheeler on Monday morning about 11 o'clock, at the office of Col. Raulston. Withers being chiefly spokesman of our committee, we stated the object of our mission, and in the name of ourselves and of our party we invited and urged them to co-operate with us in the effort to attain the desired end. They both (Wheeler and Raulston) commended our efforts as wise and prudent, and in this connection, Col. Raulston, who was then addressing himself to Col. Withers, remarked that the colored people seemed disposed not to vote at all on election day for the reason that they thought enough colored voters, on account of the riot of Saturday evening previous, had left town to cause the defeat of the Coälition ticket in Danville, and if the colored people voted they would be beaten in Danville at this election and at the next election would have to overcome the " prestige " of the Democratic victory of the 6th of November, 1883. I was on the ground a short time after the riot, and exercised myself to the best of my ability, in conjunction with other citizens, to preserve order. I never saw people under such excitement more reasonable or better disposed to obey the authority of the law. I called the meeting of the citizens at the Opera House on November 3d, 1883, to order about 3 o'clock P. M., and never saw in Danville a larger, more orderly or more representative body of Danville citizens assembled in the town, and men of all ages and avocations seemed intent upon doing all that was fair and right.

S. C. BERKELEY, Jr.

J. D. Blair, being first duly sworn, deposes and says :

I was elected a member of the council of this city at the May election, 1882 ; my term of office to commence 1st July following and continuing two years from that date. Said council was composed of twelve members, a majority of whom were Readjusters or Coalitionists, four of whom were negroes. At the organization of the council, I was elected president of that council. The police force, consisting of one chief and nine members for active duty, was elected by this body for six months at a time. At the election held about this time, for the police force, a white Coalitionist was elected chief, and one negro was placed on the regular force. I never knew one elected before in this city. The other seven members were white men. I do not now remember distinctly their political opinions, but among them was Mr. R. M. Laurie and B. F. Morrisett (Democrats), who had for a number of years been efficient policemen. The clerk of the market, elected for one year, with powers of policeman on the market, was a negro ; and the sanitary policeman elected was a negro. At the same election three Readjusters were elected aldermen, one of whom was a negro, and entered upon their duties at the same time of the council—these being all the magistrates the city was entitled to. The chief of police resigned in a short time, and a white Coalitionist was elected in his stead. At the same election, an independent candidate, endorsed by the Coalitionists, was elected mayor. These constitute the principal officers for the preservation of the peace and for the protection of the rights of citizens in this city. I think the election of many of these officers, and the course pursued by them while in office, had a tendency to make the negroes very self-asserting, and to some extent intolerant, in their conduct towards the white people. It was a common rumor some time after this period, that the chief of police, in discharging his duties, threw as much as possible of the business growing out of the police duty, before the negro magistrates. Matters continued about the same as to officers until the 1st July, 1883, at which time an election was held by the council, in which one additional negro was placed upon the police force, which made two negroes on the regular police force in addition to the sanitary policeman and clerk of the market. It was a noticable fact that at this election, that in selecting members of the police force the principal qualification appeared to me to be their political affiliation, without regard to any fitness for the office; indeed, a short time afterwards a leading Coälitionist admitted to me that the police force was elected for political reasons to contribute to the building up of the "Coälition" and "Liberal party of the State." Lawrie and Morrisett, the two most efficient members of the force, were defeated for no reason known to me, except their political opinions, and such was admitted to me to be the case by one of the leading Coälitionists (member of the council) as to Morrisett. Believing that this action by a majority of the council would tend to make the negroes become still more intolerant, and have less regard for the rights of citizens, and would engender a state of feeling that would disturb the peace and quietude of the city, and I feared it would lead to bad results, as the negroes, in many instances, seemed to think that nobody except themselves were entitled to some of the rights of citizenship, I tendered my resignation as president of the council, which was accepted at its August meeting, 1883, thereby relieving myself of holding an office in said council after I had found out that I could exercise no influence to stop this state of things, but remained a member of said body. Colonel J. B. Raulston, a leading Coälitionist, was then elected president of the council, and continued to hold said office until after the recent election. Added to all these things a fierce political contest was commenced about the 1st of September last, which contributed very much to make the negroes intolerant, insulting, and exceedingly obnoxious in their manner and ways toward the white people, until on Friday night, 2d of November, W. E. Sims, the Coälition candidate for the Senate from this senatorial district, made the most inflammatory and abusive speech—a part of which I heard—in which he abused some of the leading citizens of this city to a very great extent. I came on the street next morning early, and it was soon apparent that Sims' speech had very much aroused and excited the negroes; that whilst he had abused many of the whites in a very outrageous manner, they had acted with great forbearance and did not desire to be aggressors as to commence any conflict, but it was decided by leading men of the Democratic party that the best thing to be done was to quietly hold a meeting at half-past two o'clock that evening in the Opera House, and pass resolutions condemning Sims' inflammatory and incendiary speech, and to contradict other mis-representations. I was in said meeting, which was a very large and representative one of the white people of this city. During the progress, and before it had adjourned, firing of pistols was heard upon the streets, and persons commenced to leave the meeting. I came out later and found that a riot had occurred and was about ended. I was totally unarmed, having nothing but a small knife about me. I heard others say the same. I was in the city until after the close of the polls on the day of election. The city was policed by a number of our best citizens, under the authority of the Mayor, as I understood, with a view to protect the lives and property of our citizens, without interfering or molesting anybody that was peaceable and quiet. During the early part of Saturday night I heard firing from the outskirts of the city, and proceeded to the place where I heard it; it was just beyond the corporate limits, and ascertained that four of said police force of citizens, riding quietly along the public road, were fired into with several shots from negroes in ambush, and one of the white men wounded. The negroes were behind the house and protected so that they could not be hurt. I saw the negro that occupied the house, who admitted that the firing was done from his yard by negroes who came from a store near by, but claimed not to know who they were. A negro was arrested a short time after by the police force that I was with and a portion of the military company, armed with a pistol, with some of its barrels empty, and placed in jail to await civil trial, and I learned he has since been turned loose. On election day the city was very quiet. I saw no disposition whatever to interfere with any person qualified to vote from casting his ballot as he might elect. At the precinct at which I was most of the day, a colored man was there with Coälition tickets, and circulated around the polls as he chose without any disposition on the part of anybody, as far as I could see, or believe, to disturb him.

J. D. BLAIR.

On leaving the Opera House and the meeting I proceeded to my office on Main street, a short distance above, and learned that a considerable part of the firing and conflict during said riot occurred just opposite my office or the office of my firm, Ruffin, Woolfolk & Blair. None of the members of the firm were in said office, and only one clerk, W. J. Dance. I learned from him that the negroes were massed on Main street in front of said office, and that a few of the whites were on the sidewalk immediately in front of said office. I examined the front wall of the office and found several holes made by bullets, which could only have been shot from the negroes. I cannot now state distinctly how many, but am satisfied that there are two and probably more of such holes.

J. D. BLAIR.

The above testimony was taken, subscribed and sworn to before me on the dates above indicated.

F. F. BOWEN, N. P.

S. S. Kent, resident of Halifax county, Va., and farmer, being first duly sworn, deposes and says:

On Sunday, November 4, 1883, my son, Dr. S. T. A. Kent, heard a negro at Poden's store, in Halifax county, say, in speaking of the election in Danville, that he expected to wade up to his neck in blood. The negro was a resident of Danville, and was coming to Danville the next day to be present and vote on the day of election, November 6, 1883. My son told me the negro's name who made the foregoing declaration, but I have forgotten the name. He was, however, one of the Barksdale negroes.

S. S. KENT.

November, 21st 1883.

Capt. J. H. Oliver, being first duly sworn, deposes and says:

I live in Danville and am captain of the "Danville Grays." I was in Danville the day of the riot. I was in the store of Nicholas & Hessburg, and some one ran in and remarked that C. P. Noell had been cut to pieces by Hense Lawson. Noell being a sergeant in my company, and intimate friend, I ran at once to find out the nature of his wounds, if there were any. I found him in front of the office of Ruffin, Woolfolk & Blair, two or three doors from Nicholas & Hessburg's, surrounded by a few white men and a great many negroes. I passed through the crowd as rapidly as possible to Mr. Noell. From inquiries from him I found that he was not seriously hurt. Walter Withers (colored policeman), with my assistance, and I think Walters Holland, insisted on the negroes dispersing, who had then assembled in a great mass. In this endeavor we left the sidewalk, on which we had been standing, and went into the street, insisting that the crowd should disperse, and

I told them that if they would disperse I would guarantee the whites who were there would leave. Seeing that this effort was useless, I returned to about the position I first occupied on the sidewalk. As soon as I reached the sidewalk and faced to the street, the crowd seemed to have partially divided, the colored people in a great mass occupying the street and partially surrounding the position occupied by the white people, who were on the sidewalk in front of the office of Ruffin, Woolfolk & Blair, as aforesaid. About the centre of the circle which had been formed by the colored people was standing two large colored men, neither of which I knew, who seemed to be the principal actors on behalf of the colored people. One of them remarked : " There are the two damned scoundrels who instigated this trouble ; " and I understood him to say that " we dare them to came out."

About that time Mr. Taylor, who had been standing in my rear among the few white people that had gathered there, as well as I recollect, stepped to my right, and Mr. Geo. Lea to my left. I knew not at the time why these two gentlemen had been singled out, but learned afterwards that it was due to some part they had taken in the difficulty between Noell and Lawson. I understood one of these negroes to say that " we had as well end this matter here as any where else," and thereupon drew his pistol and afterwards the firing commenced. This was in an instant. This was the first pistol I saw immediately before the firing commenced. There had been pistols drawn before, but it had all quieted down during the endeavor of the police to disperse the crowd. A second or so after the firing commenced I saw young Holland approach the pavement almost in a line with Geo. Lea, and a negro shoot in that direction. I saw that Holland was hit. He wheeled about half face to the left and fell on the pavement some 10 or 15 feet from where I was standing. I believe that the shot was intended for Geo. Lea, as he had been invited out and it was made in a line with him, I thought. As soon as Holland fell, with the assistance of Mr. John Miller, we carried him into H. D. Guerrant & Co.'s store, a few paces above the point at which he fell. I then went as fast as I could to the armory of the " Danville Grays," to await any orders that might come from the Mayor or Sergeant to call out the company to assist either of them to quell the disturbance. Immediately I was ordered out by the Sergeant. I gave the alarm known to the company, and in a few minutes had in ranks 35 or 40 men on the streets subject to the orders of the Sheriff. They were stationed in squads, under officers of the company, upon all the streets approaching Main, where the difficulty arose, with sentinels walking the streets between the posted positions of each squad, with orders to disperse all crowds and not to allow over three men to assemble at any one place. By this means all crowds were dispersed and quiet was quickly restored upon the streets.

The company was on military duty until Monday evening, when I was directed by the Sergeant to dismiss my company, as he thought that everything was quiet, and that he would have no further use for them; that with the regular police and special police there would be no further trouble. Thereupon I dismissed the company. A few minutes after the dismissal of the company, I was ordered by Mayor Johnston to call out the company in arms and hold them in readiness in the armory, subject to his orders, and to aid the citizens, who had been appointed special police, in keeping the peace and everything quiet, and to send squads or the whole to whatever point it might be necessary for this purpose. They were sent to different parts of the city, wherever it was deemed necessary. The company was on duty until after the election, and there being no disturbance of any nature whatever, I thereupon dismissed the company by order of Major Carter, who had been sent by the Governor, with written orders to me to obey his instructions.

J. H. OLIVER.

The above testimony of the following witnesses, to wit: W. J. Dance, Chas. D. Noell, P. Bouldin, J. C. Reagen, B. F. Williamson, T. E. Gregory, J. G. Miller, Sr., L. L. Bass, Chas. Friend, Jas. P. Harrison, James Wood (Sergeant), Mason Arrington (colored), W. J. Moore, E. Keen, Jr., Dr. M. E. Douglass, Walter S. Withers (colored police), Geo. W. Swain, J. D. Blair, Capt. J. H. Oliver, Ro. Lipscomb, W. G. Lynn, W. P. Graves, J. E. Perkinson, Frank Corbett (colored), W. A. Meeks, J. T. Morton, S. F. Terry, N. F. Reid, R. M. Hubbard, H. A. Cobbs, P. B. Booth, Chas. G. Freeman (police), F. B. Fitzgerald, W. R. Taylor, Abram Wimbish, L. C. Berkley, Jr., and S. S. Kent, was taken, subscribed, and sworn to before me on the days above indicated.

Given under my hand and official seal this 21st day of November, 1883.

F. F. BOWEN, N. P.

[SEAL.]

*State of Virginia, Town of Danville, to wit:*

I, William Rison, clerk of the Hustings Court of the town of Danville, in the State of Virginia, hereby certify that F. F. Bowen is a notary public in and for the said town, duly commissioned and qualified according to law ; that he was qualified as such in said court, on the 4th day of January, 1882, his commission bearing date on the 22d day of December, 1881, and continuing for four years thereafter.

In testimony of which I hereto subscribe my name as clerk as aforesaid, and affix my seal of office this 20th day of November, in the year 1883.

WILLIAM RISON,
*Clerk of the Hustings Court of Danville, Va.*

[SEAL.]

## THE RICHMOND MILITARY IN DANVILLE.

REPORT OF THE OFFICERS IN RELATION TO THE CONDUCT OF
THE PEOPLE ON ELECTION DAY.

A few days ago Capt. Andrew Pizzini, of the Richmond Light Infantry Blues, received a letter from Maj. W. T. Sutherlin, chairman of the Committee of Forty, appointed at a meeting of citizens of Danville to collect and prepare for publication the causes of the recent riot, requesting the officers commanding the military ordered to Danville by the Governor to furnish the committee a statement containing such facts as they could justify in relation to the conduct of the people of Danville on the day of election; and also the opportunities afforded for a full vote at the polls, with any other facts they had in their possession bearing upon the subject.

The officers met yesterday for the purpose of taking action on the communication, and the following letter was sent to Major Sutherlin last evening :

RICHMOND, November 16, 1883.

*Major W. T. Sutherlin, Chairman, &c.:*

Dear Sir—In response to the request contained in yours of November 12th, the undersigned beg leave to state that under orders from his Excellency the Governor (see Special Orders No. 14 and letter of instructions, as published in Richmond and Danville papers November 6th), we arrived in Danville on the 6th instant at about 5 A. M. We found the entire town so quiet as to convey the impression that all the people were asleep.

Maj. Carter reported to the City Sergeant as soon as that officer could be found. The entire command was then disembarked and quartered into barracks of the Danville Grays. It was then so apparent that there would be no trouble in the town that Maj. Carter relieved the Danville Grays and allowed them to go to their homes for rest and refreshment.

We had ample opportunity during the entire day to observe the temper, spirit and conduct of all classes of the people, both at the polls and at their places of business and on the streets, and can testify that there was not the slightest disposition manifested by any one to commit any breach of law or order ; but, on the other hand, it was aparent that all were resolved to avoid any violence of act or word. No one was hindered from the free exercise of the right of suffrage, but, on the contrary, it was noticeable that there was a sincere desire on the part of the whites that a full vote should be polled by both political parties.

In addition to the protection afforded by the general disposition of the people, there was present a sufficient military force to enable the civil officers to protect and if necessary to enforce the rights of all citizens desiring to exercise the right of suffrage, and the whole command was ready to execute the orders of the commanding officer, who was especially enjoined to see that all persons were protected in their life, person, property, and the peaceful exercise of their lawful rights.

Any and every voter might have had complete protection from the military by simple request at any time.

This fact was made known to the voters of all classes and parties by Major Carter in person, who visited the precincts and made public announcement that he was prepared to give immunity from violence to all citizens without regard to class or party.

Crowds of citizens of both races and parties freely commingled on the streets in converse with each other and with the troops without the slightest apprehension of danger, and prominent men of both political parties repeatedly assured the officers and men of the military force that there was not the slightest necessity for their presence, as, all things considered, there was never a more quiet and peaceably disposed community, both parties having united in the determination to have complete submission to the law and its officers, and to mutually aid in its enforcement.

HENRY C. CARTER,

Major, &c., Commanding.

ANDREW PIZZINI, JR.,

Captain Commanding Richmond L. I. Blues.

BEAUREGARD LORRAINE,

Lieutenant Commanding Richmond Howitzers.

E. D. STARKE,

Captain and Ins. Artillery.

CARLTON McCARTHY,

Captain and Adjutant First Battalion Artillery.

www.ingramcontent.com/pod-product-compliance
Lightning Source LLC
Chambersburg PA
CBHW021430090426
42739CB00009B/1432